More Butterfly Moments

by Joyce B. Royals

John 3:30

Book Dedication

This book is dedicated to my husband, Andy, the love of my life, and a real encourager to me; to my children, Tina and Steve, through whom God has blessed me abundantly; and to the memory of my mother, Norma Seward Beeson, who loved me unconditionally and who was the first to teach me about Jesus.

Table of Contents

Introduction

From what at first appears its tomb
the transformed worm revives
and takes its flight on graceful wings
to soar in boundless skies
— so, too, shall I!

Butterfly Moments

Many situations in life seem overwhelming — even hopeless. Sometimes I'm compelled to write because of situations I (or someone I know) might be facing. As I put my feelings about these situations into words, God often brings reminders of His faithfulness to me. He reminds me through my hopelessness, burdens, and inadequacies of His faithfulness and love. He is working everything out for my good. I just need to trust Him. I call these reminders from Him "butterfly moments." Just as God transforms a lowly caterpillar into a beautiful butterfly, He can and will transform His child. I praise him for "butterfly moments."

Grief and Loss

Beyond Description

Could you describe the sunrise
to someone blind from birth? —
What words could help him comprehend
the colors of the earth?
How could you explain to one
the song a robin sings
if never had he heard a sound
upon his eardrum ring?
How could you define true love
in words of earthen tone
to one who'd always lived his life
abandoned and alone?
These things would be impossible —
no way could they be done! —
and neither can the mind of man
grasp all that God has done.
For earthly beauty can't begin
with Heaven to compare —
beyond description is that Home
that God's for us prepared!

Beyond the Rainbow

The sun through raindrops shines its rays
in awesome tinted hues
and paints a rainbow in the clouds
for all the world to view.
Red and orange, yellow, green,
blue, violet, indigo...
just what's beyond the pretty arc
I'd really like to know.
Gazing at the tinted sky
I wonder what you see
in Heaven's perfect land
so far away from me.
For you reside within that place
that lies beyond the bow —
and while I wonder what's beyond —
you already know!

Blest

If I could have you back again
for just a little while
I'd fill each moment with the things
I know would make you smile.
I'd tell you that I love you —
that you mean the world to me...
that you and I together
is how life ought to be.
I'd say "You make me happy —
let's share an ice cream cone;
let's sit and watch the sunset
and ignore the ringing phone."
We could reminisce and laugh awhile —
hold hands and take a walk...
pick some flowers, take a ride,
then go home and talk.
I wouldn't fret o'er little things —
nor grumble if it rained;
complain about life's problems,
nor its heartaches, trials, and pain.
But I can't bring you back to me
yet soon I'll come to you —
and in Heaven what a time we'll have
and oh, the things we'll do!
Until then I'll count myself as blest
and thank the Lord above
that I've known the very special joy
of having you to love.

Change of Address

I've moved from Earth to Heaven
and I wish that you could see
the beauty of this glorious place
that's mine eternally.
Every detail's carefully planned —
just right in every way;
songs of celebration ring
throughout the cloudless day.
There is no war nor danger
no trials and no stress...
no moan of pain, no crying,
no sorrow, and no death.
No storm can mar the atmosphere —
thieves can't enter in;
time here doesn't matter —
and praises never end.
Everything's perfection —
I don't want for anything;
Earth's problems are now over
and with angel choirs, I sing.
Best of all I dwell with Christ
and those He saved by grace —
where "good-byes" are never needed
in our perfect dwelling place!

Don't Believe It

The day may come when folks will view my body
and they'll even say that I am dead and gone,
but let me tell you now while I'm still with you —
I'll be safe and well with God in my new home.

I'll leave behind all temporal pain and sorrow —
my earthly tent I'll lay aside that day;
I'll dwell where there's eternal "Son"-shine
and the tears I shed will all be wiped away.

I'll talk again with loved ones gone before me
and what a grand reunion that will be!
We'll shout and sing eternal praise to Jesus
as we worship Him beside the crystal sea.

So if you hear that I'm no longer living,
don't believe it, but please know it isn't true;
I'll be more alive than you have ever seen me
there with Jesus where I'll someday welcome you!

Don't Forget

When my loved one died the weight of grief
seemed more than I could bear
but you're a friend who took the time
to show me that you care.
Words you spoke were comforting —
as was your gentle touch —
and for all you did to ease my pain
I thank you very much.
But today my house is empty
and I'm sitting here alone
wondering how I'll ever find
the strength to carry on.
Please now don't forget me,
visit when you can,
if speech for you is difficult
just sit and hold my hand.
If you're prone to pen a line or two
I'd love to get some mail —
or what a caring call would mean
mere words can never tell...
but if you cannot write or call
nor stop to visit me —
please pray that God will in my heart
bring peace and victory!

Don't Grieve for Me

Don't grieve for me, I'm doing fine —
　　all is perfect here;
　songs of praise from angel choirs
　　fill the atmosphere.
　The river water's crystal clear —
　　streets are purest gold;
　the tree of life bears plenteous fruit
　　and no one here grows old.
　My Heavenly body's free of pain —
　　no weakness it allows;
　I'm better than I've ever been —
　　all suffering's over now!
I live with loved ones gone before —
　　know Peter, talk with Paul;
　I see my Saviour face to face
　　and worship Him in awe.
　Real joy and perfect peace I have
　　and nothing do I lack —
　　if you could see me as I am
　　you'd never wish me back!
　Because I placed my faith in Christ
　　fore'er with Him I'll dwell;
so please don't grieve, but rest assured
　　that I'm alive and well!

Empty Arms

I'd planned to hold you in my arms
and hoped to watch you grow;
I'd thought I'd teach you how to live
and dreamed of where we'd go.
I'd imagined taking strolls with you
and singing lullabies;
I'd longed to have the time and chance
to soothe away your cries.
But now I sit here rocking
in a chair reserved for you —
with empty arms and aching heart
there's nothing I can do.
For the angels came and took you
to the Father up above,
and I know you're well and happy
in that land of perfect love.
Yet, Little One, I miss you
and am filled with grief's cruel pain;
for ever since you went away
life's pointless and seems vain.
But time will heal the hurt, I pray
and I will smile again;
God will grant me strength to cope
and bring His peace within.
So, though my arms are empty
and my eyes o'erflow with tears —
within my heart's a cradle
where I'll always hold you near!

Home

Long I'd been trapped in a world filled with hurt
where the darkness surrounded my soul;
but now I am free — truly free — of all pain —
I'm at Home and I'm healthy and whole!

I've said my "hellos" to loved ones I'd missed —
they cheered as I enter the gate;
words can't describe this Wonderful Place —
there's no darkness, no fear, and no hate.

I wriggle my toes in the River of Life
and laugh as I walk streets of gold;
my vision is perfect; the Son always shines;
and no one in Heaven is old!

So Dear One, don't grieve when I come to your mind —
smile, and with joy travel on;
trust Jesus and know that when earth's life is past —
I'll be waiting to welcome you Home!

I Know Now

If I'd known then what I know now
I would have told you once more
how much I love you.
I'd have given you another hug
and held you tight
and somehow tried to make you understand
that because of you
life was full and rich —
and ever so much more interesting!
I would have thanked you for the joy you gave
and the laughter we shared.
I'd have opened my heart
and asked forgiveness for my failures
But...
I didn't know then
that my world would soon collapse
nor that small things I'd taken for granted
would be lost forever
except in my memory.
That day seemed like any other
and I didn't know
that it would be the last we'd share.
I didn't know that my life would change completely
in one moment —
that things that once seemed so important
would cease to matter at all.
I didn't know that unbearable pain
would be the price of loss
nor that love is worth any cost —
but I know now...
and if I could live my life over again
I'd make sure to share with you
what I know now.

It's Not Good-bye

I'd grown tired of pain and trials
so my Lord said, "Come on Home;"
I closed my eyes and woke again
before the Father's throne.
I watched in rapt attention
as beside me stood God's Son...
then I heard the words I'd waited for —
"My beloved child, well done!"
I stand in awe of Christ my Lord
and all He's done for me...
and what a time I'm having here
beside the crystal sea!
My body's well; my soul at peace;
my heart feels no despair;
'midst jasper walls and gates of pearl
I live without a care!
I listen as the angels sing
and talk with saints of old;
I reminisce with Paul and John
and walk on streets of gold.
Be thankful that my suffering's o'er —
that from Earth's bonds I'm free;
if you could only see me now
you'd be so glad for me!
So don't you grieve, it's not "Good-bye" —
be patient for a while...
and when you enter Heaven's gates
I'll greet you with a smile!

Not Grieving

It happened gradually,
a thief crept into your life,
muddled your thoughts,
and chipped away at your dignity.
You couldn't remember where you lived
or where you'd parked
or even if you'd eaten,
Tasks you'd always done easily
went undone, skills forgotten.
I looked at you and saw a stranger...
yet there were precious moments
when you'd come back to me,
speak my name
and share some special thought.
But these times grew fewer and farther apart.
Your bewildered look announced
that you didn't know me.
Little by little I lost you.
Although I could hold your hand
I could no longer touch your soul.
I wept...
But today there's no reason to cry.
I celebrate.
You've laid aside earth's hindrances and moved to Heaven.
Your mind is clear and your body perfect.
What a time you must be having!
Although I miss you, I'm not grieving...
I did that when I lost the real you long ago.
Now I can only feel relief that you've been set free.
I rejoice in knowing that someday we'll be together again.
You'll speak my name
and we'll both understand the "whys" of life's difficulties...

but it won't matter anymore.
There'll be no Alzheimer's, no grief, no pain —
just joy and peace and love!
Good-bye for now.
I love you.

Reality

Today when I woke, I hoped I'd simply had a bad dream.
I willed you to walk through the door.
I listened for your voice and anticipated your smile...
but
reality soon seared my consciousness.
My heart was filled with the unbearable ache of loneliness.
I realized there would be no more mornings of family breakfasts
nor
lazy evenings of shared laughter over nothing
...and everything
I think back.
It was a day like any other.
No premonition whispered that it would be different
nor warned that it would be the last I'd share with you.
How could I have taken you so for granted?
It's the simple, unspoken things I miss —
the staunch allegiance we felt for each other...
the mutual acceptance of faults and failures...
the appreciation of strengths and victories.
I long for the opportunity to tell you once again how very important
you were to me...
how much I cherished you...
how much I owe to you...
Yet somehow, I think you know.
You changed my life;
you're still a big part of who I am.
Because you're gone
nothing will ever be the same.
You left a void no one else can fill —
but
the memory of your love will sustain me.

I can never again take life for granted.
I'll hold each memory as a treasure of immeasurable worth
and view each moment as an opportunity
because I now know how quickly someone can be snatched away.
Without a doubt
loving you was worth the pain of missing you.
No, this isn't a bad dream, no matter how I may wish it were so.
This is reality: life must go on without you.
You'd want it that way.
I'll claim God's help and move ahead
with a thankful heart that for a time
I had the joy and privilege
of
sharing life with you!

Remember Me

Remember me, but go on with your life —
there's really no need to grieve;
I simply moved out of my earthly abode
when God said 'twas time to leave.
My new Home is perfect, I'm happy and well —
I sing in the Heavenly choir;
peace, joy, and love fill the atmosphere
and angels grant every desire.
Rest assured that I love you with all of my heart
and cherish the times that we shared;
my life was enriched by your thoughtfulness
and the ways that you showed me you cared.
Recall all the times that we walked hand-in-hand —
treasure sweet memories;
cry as you must, but then praise the Lord
that from pain and trials I'm free!
I'll greet you someday on Heaven's sweet shore
where together we'll worship our Lord —
then you'll see for yourself that God's promise is true —
Heaven's worth waiting for!

Reminisce and Smile

Please listen as I share some words
I hope will comfort you;
you're struggling with this time of grief
but you will make it through.
God chose the hour to call me home
and He makes no mistake;
He'll give you strength to move ahead
and guide each step you take.
Please dry your tears and don't be sad;
I'm truly well and whole;
without a care, on golden streets
with loved ones I now stroll.
With songs of praise I worship Christ...
life is full and good;
you wouldn't want to call me back —
even if you could!
But someday when you join me here
I'll take you by the hand
and we'll explore the wonders
of this perfect heav'nly land.
So until then please live by faith —
don't worry 'bout a thing;
waste no time on past regrets —
trust God with everything.
And it's okay to stop at times
and reminisce awhile —
then what I really hope you'll do
is think of me and smile!

The Empty Space

I've survived my share of battles —
God's grace has brought me through;
at times I've been quite overwhelmed
and not known what to do.
My body's been assaulted —
my mind o'ercome by stress,
at times my faith has grown quite weak,
and oft' I've been distressed.
But now I find I'm in a place
I've never walked before —
the empty space inside my heart
I simply can't ignore.
I don't understand the "why"
of this great loss to me,
and how I'll face the days ahead
I really cannot see.
Now tho' the pain of loneliness
seems more than I can bear,
and tho' I'm overcome by grief
I'll turn to God in prayer.
He's promised He won't leave me —
His mercies never cease;
in time He'll fill the empty space
with His amazing peace!

Transformed!

From earthen sod, a tiny seed
becomes a mighty oak;
a butterfly emerges from
a worm's confining cloak.
A robin hatches from an egg —
a babe comes from the womb;
and Jesus Christ came forth alive
from a borrowed tomb.
Because my Savior conquered death
I, too, have victory —
and when I lay this body down
a new one awaits for me!
Someday I'll close my eyes and walk
through Heaven's open door —
and there transformed with Christ my Lord
I'll live forevermore!

Welcome Home

I didn't want to leave you
but I'd grown tired and slow;
then when Jesus called my name
I knew that I must go.
I ran right in through Heaven's gate
and looked around in awe —
and let me tell you, there's no way
to tell you all I saw!
An angel escort guided me
along the streets of gold
where loved ones took me by surprise
for none of them was old!
"Welcome home," they said with glee
"you sure are looking well!
"We're awfully glad that you've arrived
in Heav'n with us to dwell!"
They pointed me to Jesus' throne —
I fell upon my knees —
and raised my hands in praise to Him
for all He's done for me.
I'm feeling great, my body's whole,
I've lots of energy —
and from every earthly pain and grief
I'm now completely free!
So Dear One, please don't wish me back
someday you'll come to me —
Then "Welcome Home," I'll say to you
throughout eternity!

Difficult Times

Adrift

Bobbing about on the face of the sea —
at times covered over by surf,
the miniscule cork is tossed to and fro
away from the surety of turf.
Perpetually moving, but going nowhere,
in circles when calm is the sea...
pounded and hurled by furious waves
when storms grow as fierce as can be.
Through calmest of waters and roughest of waves
it endures long days and dark nights,
ceaselessly drifting alone in the deep —
hopeless and endless its plight.
Like a weathered cork in the deepest sea
too tiny to touch ocean's bed —
day after day I'm carried along —
adrift — but not moving ahead.
Hoping for rescue but knowing not how,
overwhelmed by deep waves of care
I search God's dear word and find just the hope
to lift me from seas of despair.
For I have the promise that I'm NOT alone —
God's placed me here in the swells...
and I'm secure for He masters the seas,
and His Spirit in me surely dwells.
So, I need not fear the waves and the winds —
my Heavenly Father's their source...
and I'm not adrift in the ocean of life,
my Lord's carefully charted my course!

Anchored

All around me dreams have crumbled —
hopes lie shattered in the dust;
pressures mount from all directions...
is there nothing I can trust?
Things I'd thought would stand life's pressures
cannot still the storms that rage;
all Earth's "sureties" I'd thought certain
one by one have passed away.
Doubts and weakness plague my pathway —
fears assault my heart and mind;
for life's overwhelming questions —
answers I can't seem to find.
Yet I know my Lord can't fail me
tho' I'm feeling worn and stressed —
anchored where life's storms can't shake me
in my Savior I find rest.

Blessing in Disguise

Do you ever feel discouraged,
tired, helpless, and alone?
Do you sometimes cry to God in prayer
for the strength to carry on?
Have you ever faced a hurtful trial
and not known what to do?
Are you dwelling in a valley
wondering how you'll make it through?
Every path of pain you tread
is paved with God's great love;
each heartache draws your eyes of faith
to the Father's throne above.
So let me now encourage you
to run this earthly race
in a way your life will show each day
God's presence, love, and grace.
No difficulty comes your way
that takes God by surprise —
each burden that you bear He'll make
a blessing in disguise.

Broken Promise

I promised the Lord to be faithful to Him
and with all of my heart was sincere;
I thought that no matter what I'd stay true —
for His presence to me was so near.
But soon I discovered that problems arose
and their purpose I just couldn't see;
feeling abandoned, alone, and confused
I feared what would happen to me.
No longer by faith, but by feelings, I lived —
forsaking the vow that I'd made...
knowing I'd failed, all my hopes dashed to bits,
I was despondent and feeling afraid.
But deep in my heart a Voice quietly said,
"My child, you need not despair;
your faults and your failures were nailed to the cross —
all forgiven, so leave them there!
"You've broken your promise, but lean now on Me —
my plan for your life is success;
I'll never forsake you, I'm true to My word —
secure in My love you can rest!"

Choices

Should I "throw in the towel" and simply give up?
Should I walk away from the fight?
I'm tired of battling untruths and deceit
in the struggle to do what is right.
Day after day I start over again
determined to be loving and kind;
I try to treat others with love and respect
but in turn am betrayed and maligned.
Who can I trust? Where should I turn?
How do I know what to do?
Things may look hopeless and I feel alone
but Lord, I'll keep trusting in You.
Help me to walk in the path that You choose —
remove all my doubts and each fear;
teach me to pray for Your will, not mine,
remind me that You always hear.
Forgive my complaints; mold every thought;
guard all that I say and do;
fill me with wisdom so choices I make
will always lead others to You.

Focus

When I look around at what goes on
I'm prone to grow distressed;
war and famine, hatred, crime —
this world is in a mess!
Satan smiles and says to me,
"There's nothing you can do!"
But I'll not look at circumstance,
Dear Lord, I'll look to You!
For You're the One Who guides my steps
tho' dark and vile the night;
You're the One when all else fails
with power to set things right.
You're the One Who gives sweet peace
when I'm on bended knee —
and You're the One who fights for me
assuring victory.
I know that You, through me will do
what I alone can't do
when I don't look at circumstance
but focus, Lord, on You!

For Such a Time

What problem are you facing now
where you must make the choice
to stand with courage for the right
and boldly raise your voice?
You know down deep within your heart
what God demands of you —
and yet it seems you've much to lose
if His will you do.
Recall how Esther trusted God —
risking everything
and saved a nation when she pled
for mercy from the King.
Take heart, although the task be great
and don't its blessings miss;
for God has surely placed you here
for such a time as this!

God Brought Good

My heart is plagued by "might-have-beens,"
"if-onlys" and "I wish;"
I'm prone to question, "What's the point?"
and "What will come of this?"
I cannot comprehend this grief,
not understand its "Why?";
I pine for "what-I-hoped-would-be" —
and for its loss I cry.
But I can't change my yesterdays
nor relive what is past;
I needn't weep o're broken dreams
nor for their purpose ask.
But I can trust my Lord today
and claim His strength to cope —
I know He'll help me walk by faith
and fill my heart with hope.
I'll rest in His unfailing love
and someday I will see
how from this overwhelming pain
God brought good for me.

God's in Control

I'm scared and overwhelmed right now
and don't know what to do;
my mind is tired, emotions stretched,
my body's worn out, too.
The day ahead seems frightening —
things really seem a mess;
I feel this hour helpless
and panicked, I confess.
But I'll hang on to promises
my Father's made to me;
I have His word, He's in control
and leads me faithfully.
Not one thing surprises God —
no fear, no grief, nor pain;
He's in control, so I'm assured
He'll from this trial bring gain.
So when life brings cruel circumstance
and round me troubles roll,
I'll cast out doubt, for I'm assured —
God's fully in control!

Going Through the Motions

I'm just going through the motions
trying to survive;
my body's tired, my schedule's full,
my mind's in overdrive.
Hoping I can do things well —
not seeing any way,
wondering how I'll find the strength
to make it through the day.
I often grow forgetful
for there's much I need to do;
sometimes confusion claims my thoughts
and I don't have a clue.
I often feel that I can't cope
with all life's daily "stuff";
it seems no matter what I do
it never is enough!
So I'll depend upon the One
Who loves and cares for me;
my Heavenly Father hears my cry
and listens patiently.
He knows exactly what I need —
and all I need He'll give...
that I won't simply "make it through"
but each day fully live.

His Promise

Crushed by life's burdens
bewildered I cry;
tho' I beg for sweet respite
relief is denied.

My world seems in shambles —
I question, "Lord why?"
I listen for answers
but hear no reply.

Yet I think of past times
when my faith has been tried;
through each my Lord kept me
so gloom I'll deny.

I'll trust Him Who's faithful —
on His word I'll rely;
His promise is sure —
what I need He'll supply.

In Him

God loves me enough to place me here
in a valley that's empty and grim —
where there seems no hope and no purpose —
unless I look only to Him.

I can't see an end to this trial
and any chance of relief appears slim,
but my Lord's in control of the outcome
and I can rely upon Him.

He's patiently guiding my footsteps
and tho' light for the journey grows dim —
I'll still praise Him for time in this valley
because my faith is in Him.

In the Desert

In the past, I've sung praises to Jesus
in awe of His workings and plan —
feeling His Spirit within me —
aware of His masterful hand.

But I find myself now in the desert —
unsure why God's placed me here...
longing for flower-filled meadows
where showers of ease persevere.

Yet I've placed my faith in the Savior
and my fervent prayer He has heard;
that He'll never leave nor forsake me
is the promise of His Holy Word.

And when I reach the portals of Heaven
God's purpose I'll then understand —
so I'll trust Him here in the desert
assured that it's part of His plan.

Locked Doors

That evening they hid behind bolted doors
in fear for their very lives...
for three days had passed since Golgotha's trial
and their faith had failed to survive.
The plans they'd envisioned had faded away —
their dreams had collapsed and died;
the One they had thought would conquer their foes
instead had been crucified.
Then Jesus appeared and stood in the midst,
not hindered by locks and barred doors;
He showed them the scars in His hands and His side
so they'd need to be frightened no more.
He'd overcome Death and paid sin's great price
and returned to these that He loved
to send them to tell a lost world of God's grace
when the Spirit came down from above.
This calls to my mind the "doors" in my life
behind which I cower in fear;
the Lord knows my need and speaks to my heart
a message that I clearly hear:
"Dear Child. I am with you, don't be afraid —
there's something I want you to do;
go share My love with folks who've lost hope
and tell them I'm Faithful and True.
Be filled with My Spirit; trust in My word;
you're empowered to do this great task,
for 'locked doors' you'll see are but portals through which
I will bring the victory to pass!"

Maelstrom

Like a twig whisked about in a whirlpool
I've no choice in the path that I take —
    for swept by events fast-unfolding
    all "sureties" of life seem at stake.
I don't know where I'll be carried
and I'm helpless in stemming the tide —
    yet I have no fear of the journey
    for safe in my Lord I reside.
This maelstrom His purpose can't hinder
    for He carefully planned it for me;
    each twist and turn He has routed
    to take me where I should be.
So tho' my foundations seem shaken
    there's no reason for fear or alarm;
    I need not fear where I'm going —
    I'm safe in my Father's arms!

Refuge

I often feel quite worn and weary —
rushed and wretched, I confess;
plans collapse and dreams lie crumpled —
life around me seems a mess!
Problems mount and try my patience —
turmoil reigns on every side;
friends forsake and I try vainly
all my hurt and grief to hide.
There appears no ray of sunshine
in the long and trying days;
battles rage within my bosom
and quite hopeless seems the way.
But in the testing and the trials
I will seek my Father's heart —
where sweet peace and refuge wait me
as He makes all fears depart.
I'm assured He'll safely keep me
sheltered in His loving care
and as I rest within His presence
hope is born from deep despair.
The Lord's my Strength and precious Refuge —
to fret and worry is absurd;
I'll look to Him and not be shaken
but be still and trust His word.

My Resource

There's no going back, but the way's barred ahead —
tomorrow looks bleak and my heart's filled with dread;
I'm shrouded in darkness, yet longing for light —
hemmed in on each side with no rescue in sight.
My resources wasted; my options all gone;
helpless, defeated, and feeling alone...
afraid, tired, bewildered, and misunderstood —
helpless to change things, tho' wishing I could.
Weary of heartbreak, in anguish I cry,
"About this fierce trial, Lord, how will it end?
What must I do to see my way clear?
It's vict'ry I want, but I'm living in fear!"
Then I'm drawn to God's word where I find what I need —
as He whispers His peace when the scriptures I heed.
I read that God's love no harm will allow
and Him I can trust with the "why" and the "how."
He'll never forsake me, but holds me e'er near;
as His cherished child I've no reason to fear!
My Father's my resource, I'm safe in His hand —
I can trust in His word, tho' I don't understand!

Night Train

I lie awake in the darkness
unable to sleep.
I hear the whistle of the night train
and wonder at its mystery:
Where has it traveled?
Where is it going?
My heart searches for answers to questions
that my mind can't even put into words.
Why?
What am I missing?
What does my future hold?
What will become of me —
and of my dreams?
Where am I going?
Like the lonely wail of the night train
my heart cries out...
God hears.
He knows where I am,
where I've been,
and where I'm going.
He understands my fear...
for He has
with much love and care
laid the track
on which I travel!

No!

I sought to accomplish great things in life
and pondered the way I should go —
but I asked Him in prayer 'bout the plans I had made
and the answer He gave was a "No."
Then crushed in my spirit, bewildered, depressed
I attempted to understand...
but in searching the Scripture, no reason I found —
so, I placed it all in God's hands.
I still cannot see the "why" of it all
yet I'm sure in my heart that God knows
how to fashion me into a likeness of Him
that my life may honor Him most.
I'll worry no more, but yield to my Lord —
secure in His plan I can rest...
tho' my Heavenly Father's answer is "No" —
He's doing for me what is best!

Okay to Cry

I feel hurt and alone, tired and afraid —
bewildered by life's many cares
and I think it a sign that I'm weak and undone
if I show that I'm feeling despair.
But I sink to my knees in the dark of the night
and call to my Father above,
"Please help me, I'm frightened, I don't understand!"
and He answers in infinite love:
"Dear Child, lean on Me, claim My strength as your own,
be quiet, and give Me you cares;
you're never alone, you've no need to fear —
I'm with you and hear every prayer
"You needn't feel shame, your tears aren't in vain,
I sent them to humble your soul;
they'll lighten the load of your overwrought heart,
clear your vision and help make you whole.
"Don't worry or fret, you're safe in My arms,
and tho' you cannot see why —
when hardships arise. and answers aren't clear,
take comfort — it's okay to cry."

Promised Land

Dwelling in the wilderness
not wanting here to stay;
longing for the promised land
yet I can't see the way.
For up ahead are mountain trails
that seem too steep to climb...
and of the trek through deepest vales,
I grow afraid sometime.
But when I grow quite overwhelmed
and feel I can't go on,
I'll claim God's strength and trust in Him
Who's faithful to His own.
When the pathway to the Promised Land
at times grows rough and drear —
each step I take, Christ walks with me,
so I've no need to fear!

Sweet Victory

Dear Lord, I know I'm helpless —
there's nothing I can do;
my heart is shattered by this hurt
that I now bring to You.
Dread of what the future holds
fills me with dismay,
and seconds seem like hours
as I try to live this day.
I ask for faith that I to You
all worry may release;
calm my fears and fill my mind
with thoughts that bring me peace.
I claim Your mercy and Your grace
that I can better cope,
and grant to me Your wisdom —
for without it I've no hope!
I'm thankful that You're in control,
and someday I will see
that even from this tragedy
You'll bring sweet victory!

The Answer

I long to understand —
but knowing "why" won't change things.
I must deal with the situation.
I pray for wisdom
and my heart cries out for deliverance,
Questions plague me:
How can I find meaning in this dilemma?
How can I survive its pain?
What good can possibly come from this?
What should I do?
Where do I go from here?
The more I search for answers
the more they elude me.
Truth slowly dawns —
this is what faith is about.
If I can see, touch, or feel the answers,
it's not faith.
I pray that God will grant me faith
for I have none of my own,
Indeed, faith is a gift...
a gift which brings peace
even amidst calamities —
a gift which demands no answers.
It is anchored in the knowledge
that God makes no mistakes
and that He allows only what will work for my good.
I may still ask questions —
but only God has the answers.
Sometimes it's best that He not reveal them to me.
I can trust Him —
for ultimately
He is the Answer!

The Outcome

The heat of the battle is growing intense
and weapons are leveled at me.
What can I do that will set things aright?
No answer to this can I see.
Family and friends say I shouldn't quit
that I mustn't run from the fight —
and I really believe that wrong cannot win —
that truth will be brought to the light.
Yet I'm tired of defending myself day to day
and feeling that I stand alone...
why is the blame being placed upon me?
I'm troubled at what's going on!
But I must stand firm for all who can't fight
and what's honest and just I must choose;
I cannot afford, for truth's sake, to quit —
to bow to defeat, I refuse.
I'll pray for the courage to stand for what's right
and strength to do what I should,
and I'll trust that in time the war will be won
and the outcome will be for the good.

The Promise

Peals of thunder roll around me —
fiercest lightning stabs the sky;
howling winds express their fury
while in fear I cringe and cry.
But amidst the howls and flashes
speaks a Voice within my heart
that brings me sweet assurance
and bids all fear depart.
"Child, this storm will not destroy you —
it's intended for your gain;
tho' you wish for rays of sunshine
your barren soul's in need of rain.
You'll survive the storm's cruel fury,
I will shelter you from harm...
and you can know with full assurance
that you're safe within My arms!"

The Storm

Storm clouds fill the atmosphere —
it's dark on every side;
as thunder roars its fearsome threats
I want to run and hide.
But tho' I long to flee the storm
it seems I must remain,
for God says, "Child, I've sent this storm —
your soul requires the rain.
'Neath cloudless skies you cannot thrive —
you'd soon grow parched and dry;
please know I'd never bring you harm —
on Me you can rely!
When this storm has done its task
the darkened skies I'll clear...
and you'll then see the rainbow
that I've fashioned with your tears."

The Struggle

The plans I've made seem good and right,
but they can never be
for all's been changed by this event
which I could not foresee.
Confused about what's happening —
afraid of what's to come;
I wonder what I ought to do —
my dreams are all undone.
Worry whispers, "Just give up!"
Doubt taunts, "You can't cope!"
Logic screams, "Now think it through!"
Despair says, "There's no hope."
But I'll trust God and heed His word,
by grace my plans release
and from this struggle He'll in time
bring victory and peace!

Then I'll Understand

Stretched to the limit, disheartened, and tired,
bearing the burden of stress...
misunderstood by those I'd thought friends —
how did I get in this mess?
I search for life's meaning, but answers elude
as I question just what's going on;
pressing ahead just trying to survive
yet feeling afraid and alone.
I battle life's problems seeking their cure
often distressed and perplexed;
unsure of decisions that I need to make —
wond'ring what might happen next.
But I'll pray for the faith to weather life's storms
'til the day when they're over at last;
then I'll understand how God carefully planned
my present, my future, my past.

Tired

I'm tired of the struggles
tired of the games
tired of betrayal
tired of the pain;
exhausted of body
my heart's heavy, too,
weary of mind
can't see my way through.
Each day brings more battles
I can't seem to win
and I long for the time
they'll come to an end.
By grace I'll surrender,
Lord, fully to You
and rely on Your strength
to carry me through.

Today is Enough

As I look back, I can't figure it out.
I tried; I really did —
and yet now I find myself feeling like a failure.
Each day is a struggle.
I'm haunted by what might have been
and broken-hearted by what seems to be.
I have no control over this.
The harder I try to set things right
the worse they get.

Grief and frustration betray me.
I say the wrong thing;
I apologize repeatedly for things done with good intent
that somehow end up all wrong.
I walk on eggshells...not knowing what to do;
I wonder what will happen next.
Hurt is deep and confusion endless.
Dread plagues me.
I can't look ahead
for this moment takes all my strength.

Yet amidst all this turmoil I find hope.
My Father has promised that I'm not alone;
this is part of His plan for my life
and He knows best.
Tho' I don't understand what's going on
He'll help me accept...
and with that acceptance will come peace.
And by God's grace, I won't fear tomorrow;
I'll trust Him today —
and today is enough!

Tools

Problems abound and I feel overwhelmed
by fears that cut fiercely and deep;
turmoil and doubt fill my heart with despair
while hope and direction I seek.
Abandoned by friends I'd thought understood,
bewildered and feeling alone,
I stand at the crossroads — the pathway's unclear,
and I pray for the strength to go on.
Yet deep in my heart, I hear my Lord's voice
as He whispers, "Dear Child, I am here.
You're sealed by My Spirit, anchored in love —
there's nothing that you need to fear!
"These problems are tools that I've planned for good —
give me your worry and strife...
I'll guide every step and bring your heart peace
as you trust Me in full with your life!"

Triumph from Despair

Like Joseph alone in a wilderness pit*
taunted by doubt and fear,
I wonder if I've been abandoned
and why I've been placed in here.
Trapped on all sides by darkness,
with no hope of rescue in sight —
betrayed by those I had trusted,
I'm yearning for freedom and light.
In anguish I cry to my Father
and beg release from this place:
"Child," He whispers, "I've planned this;
to face it, I'll give you the grace.
Its purpose, in time you'll see clearly —
its outcome will surely be great;
your faith through this trial will blossom —
now trust Me and patiently wait.
I've brought you here to this cistern —
of your suffering I'm fully aware;
give thanks and know without question
that triumph I'll bring from despair!"

Genesis 37:19-24

True Riches

People that know me think all is well
for what's on my mind, my face doesn't tell.
The bills are all due, the bank account's dry —
my resources fail, and I question, "Lord, why?"
I wonder why many who don't seem to care
prosper each day while I feel despair.
As I struggle to make it, they reach the top
and so often it seems that their greed is non-stop.
I persistently try to do what is right
but pressures grow greater and no end is in sight.
Yet when I consider what life's all about
I see myself wealthy and banish all doubt.
My Father has chosen to place me right here;
since He's in control I've no need to fear.
The path where He leads is planned for my gain
tho' often it's cluttered with trials and pain.
But victory waits at the end of life's road
where my mansion's constructed in Heaven's abode.
There'll be no more problems, no sickness, no tears,
and I'll see the worth of my earthly years.
It's not what I own, nor accolades won,
but lives that are changed by deeds kindly done
hearts I encourage by showing I care —
burdens I lift and love that I share.
These are true riches, without any doubt,
for they make a difference and make my life count.

Weary

I've finally reached my limit —
my anger's grown intense!
The way I'm treated isn't fair
nor makes a bit of sense!
In spite of what I do or say,
it seems I just can't win;
folks gossip 'bout the faults I have
while my actions they condemn.
They mock the things I say and do
and think that I should change;
but if they knew the thoughts I have
they'd really think me strange!
I'm weary of their childish ways
and long to just give in —
my best is never good enough
to satisfy their whims!
To carry on, I need God's strength
I need His peace within;
He'll help me all these wrongs forgive
as I yield myself to Him.
I pray His grace will cleanse my heart
and all my thoughts control —
that His love will flow from me
and touch their troubled souls!

Whatever Comes

Dear Father, do you hear my cry?
I'm really quite confused.
I ask that You will bring me peace
through all that may ensue.
Bewildered by what's happening,
I'm hurt and feel alone;
please help me now to walk with You
and make these fears be gone.
I know it's not by accident
You've brought me to this place;
so guide my steps that folks, in me,
will see Your precious face.
My heart is broken, I'm afraid —
what's this all about?
Dear Lord, I ask that from my heart
You'll cast away all doubt.
Help me trust You totally
and use me as You will;
please give to me Your wisdom
and Your word in me instill.
I need Your grace to make it
so please my faith renew;
whatever comes, it's in Your hands —
I leave it all to You!

What's Right

Each day I try to live my life
by doing right and good;
but oft' in anger I react
and don't do as I should.
For when I look around I see
injustice and deceit
while in my heart frustration grows
as lies and greed I meet.
I wonder what will happen next —
will my best efforts fail?
When will evil tactics end
and truth in full prevail?
I'm tempted to "fight fire with fire" —
get even, be unkind —
but such behavior cannot bring
real joy nor peace of mind.
So I'll pray God will use my life
to bring His truths to light
and someday I believe that He
will make all wrong things right!

Relationships

Bank Account

What I possess in worldly goods seems paltry to my mind;
my children won't be wealthy heirs from what I'll leave behind.
I'd hoped to will them bank accounts, real estate, and bonds,
cars and homes, fancy jewels — things of which they're fond.
I'd planned a stock portfolio, life insurance, CDs
so they could have the guarantee of real financial ease.
But somehow living day-to-day has taken all I've made;
my heritage of earthly wealth is skimpy, I'm afraid.
But if I could live my life again, I'd do things much the same —
I wouldn't seek for earthly wealth or a famous name.
I'd savor every moment spent and every joy we'd share —
hugs and kisses..."I love you's"...saying bedtime prayers;
stories read on rainy days...picnics in the park...
hearty laughter...family meals...and snuggling in the dark;
cards and notes...silly songs...talks held late at night —
easing fears...drying tears...and making "boo-boos" right.
I pray my kids won't be ashamed when they remember me
and they'll not doubt I sought God's will for what He'd have me be.
I hope that they'll recall tough times when trials and hurt assailed
and see that as I trusted God, He truly never failed.
So my best assets aren't on Earth but placed in Christ instead
where they'll not rust and not decay — I'm sending them ahead!
These things within my children's hearts I want them to retain
and when I leave this world behind, may this great truth remain:

of things that really matter most
I owned a vast amount —
and being "Mom" to each of them
was my prize "bank account"!

Daughter-in-Law

When he was just a little boy
I'd watch him run and play
and in my mind I'd visualize
the wife he'd have someday.
Her smile would bring him hope and joy...
her touch would ease his pain;
her heart with his would beat as one...
her love would be his gain.
Her eyes would see into his soul
and for his faults she'd pray;
her ears would listen carefully
to what he'd try to say.
Tho' rich or poor, when sick or well,
her love would know no end...
and when the trials of life grew rough
she'd be his faithful friend.
I pictured her as in God's care
learning right from wrong —
and prayed she'd have the qualities
to make a marriage strong.
Yes, this is how I pictured what
his future bride would be;
then he grew up and brought you home
and spoke these words to me:
"Mom, here's the one I've waited for —
with whom I'll share my life;
I've asked and she's consented
to be my wedded wife."
Pride in you shone from his face,
his voice o'erflowed with joy;
the man who spoke so lovingly
was once my little boy.

Now I can't help but love you, too,
my precious daughter-in-law...
for when I pictured my son's wife —
you're the one I saw!

Forgive Them

Dear Lord,
You know that it hurts to be misunderstood
to be maligned and criticized —
gossiped about and made fun of
and not be given the chance to defend myself.
I wonder what I've done
that may have provoked this backstabbing, undermining...
and even, at times, outright contempt
by those around me.
I search my soul but can't find an answer.
Help me to treat others with respect, kindness,
and compassion
and to avoid a judgmental attitude,
remembering that I can't fully understand another person's
behavior
unless and until I've "walked in her shoes."
I pray for wisdom:
Lord, what can I do to make things better?
My heart's desire is to be a person of honesty and integrity,
who has the courage to stand up for what's right —
even when no one else will.
Help me exhibit a spirit of love and forgiveness
so that others will clearly see You in my life.
Give me the grace to yield all
I am and have
to You...
that I may be able to pray, as did Jesus,
Your Son and my Savior,
on the cross:
"Father, forgive them
for they know not what they do."
Amen.

Harvest

I'm angry and hurt at how things are done;
they're unjust, unfair, and dead wrong!
What should I do that will honor my Lord?
How long will this evil go on?
I know that the harvest will sprout from the seed —
that the crop will reveal what's been sown;
but I'm growing impatient and yearn for the time
when what's hidden by all will be known.
Now tho' I may think that enough is enough
and feel I can't take anymore —
in His own time and in His own way
God's promised He'll settle the score.
These trials are but gifts from God's loving heart
and with wisdom He's planned them for me
to fashion my life by His perfect will
into all He wants me to be.
I pray that He'll mold every thought and each deed
that my words will be tempered with love;
that the seeds of my life will yield glory and praise
to my Father in Heaven above!!

Generation Gap

What do you see when you look at me?
Do you know who I really am —
or are you distracted by my thinning white hair. wrinkled skin, and age
spots?
Do you notice that I don't move as quickly as you do
or that my steps are not always steady and sure?
Do you see that sometimes my clothes don't match?
Is that what you see?
What do you hear when I speak?
Do you notice the crackles in my voice —
do you get frustrated what I often repeat what I've just said —
or that I may ask you to repeat what you've just said to me —
or, do you even notice me at all?
Do you think I have nothing left to offer?
Does my age mean that I no longer have value?
I was once young like you, but, oh, how the years have flown —
although some nights and days have seemed to last forever!
Someday, God willing, you'll grow old, too, and you may wish
for a chance to be valued by a young friend.
Do you have any idea how much I would love to have you spend time with
me?
I look at you and long to know you better...
for when I look at you, I see promise and hope.
I see your spirit of adventure and your zest for life —
I have them too!
Sure, I probably have more aches and pains than you do —
but I'm learning to live with them
and to keep them in perspective.
If you'll help me, we can learn and do so many things together.
I'd love to hear your hopes and dreams...
I could share my experiences with you.
I'd like to teach you some lessons I've learned:

this life is only temporary —
and although its problems can seem huge at times, they WILL pass.
There's no reason to worry — worry doesn't change a thing
except it does rob you of the ability to enjoy life and deal effectively with
its
situations.
Some of life's blessings can come disguised as troubles and trials,
but NOTHING is impossible with God.
I could go on, but I'd rather you come sit with me,
let's bridge the generation gap:
let's eat ice cream together.
Let's get to know each other...
then we can really look at each other and really hear one another.
I'm a person with thoughts and feelings just like you...
one who has a desire to truly matter in your life, to really love you and be
loved by
you.
Come, young one, I'm waiting for you!

I Love You

I've heard the words, "I love you,"
and basked in sweet content —
but often later realized
they weren't sincerely meant.
For what those three small words had said
was that folks for awhile
had liked the way I spoke or looked
or pleased them with my style.
But now I've found a faithful Friend
Who's not for show or sham,
Someone on Whom I can depend
Who loves me as I am...
A Friend Who tells me when I'm wrong,
but loves me anyway,
Someone Who celebrates my joys
and through the tough times stays.
This Friend helps me face each day
by walking by my side;
He knows my hopes and calms my fears
and in Him I confide.
This Perfect Friend brings peace and joy
and faithfully teaches me
that sacrifice, forgiveness, trust...
is what "I love you" means.

If I Could

If I could I'd take upon myself
your hurts and make them mine;
I'd bear for you the dreary days
and give you brightest sunshine.
I'd fill each day with laughter...
eliminate your tears;
I'd drive away each troubling thought
and soothe away your fears.
You'd never feel rejection...
you'd not have trials nor pain;
you'd never ache with loneliness
nor want for earthly gain.
Grief would never haunt you...
no doubt would plague your mind...
and everyone with whom you deal
would be polite and kind.
Yet, in my heart I know life's storms
are sent to make us strong;
the Lord's planned each one carefully —
and we to Him belong.
So if I could, I'd grant you faith
to weather all life's tests
that you would always trust in God
to do for you what's best.

I Never Said It

I knew I should and thought I would —
but somehow didn't do it;
I put it off 'til "a better time" —
and really meant to say it!

I didn't talk to you of Christ
nor of eternity;
I didn't stop to share with you
His love for you and me.

I didn't take the time to say
you must be born again
but planned someday I'd tell you
since I said you were my friend.

The chance has passed to say it now —
and, Oh! How I regret it!
I stand ashamed with a broken heart
because I never said it.

Lift My Name

You tell me that you love me
and ask what you can do
to ease the burden that I bear
and help me make it through.
Send a card or letter,
bring a casserole,
take the time to pick me up
and take me to a show.
Call and say I'm on your mind,
visit when you can —
and if you see I'm overworked
then lend a helping hand.
Don't judge me when I stumble —
accept me as I am;
listen when I need to talk
or simply hold my hand.
Most of all each time you pray
please lift my name in prayer
and ask the Lord to use my life
His peace and love to share.

Letter from Mom

If you could step inside my heart
and all its secrets see
you'd clearly understand, my child,
how much you mean to me.
You'd view upon its every wall
scenes of times we've shared —
ups and downs — vict'ries, trials...
joys and deep despair.
You'd feel the longing of my soul
for something I could do
to have the power to change your life
and make things right for you.
You'd hear the echoes of my cries,
and all the prayers I pray;
you'd know the pain of my regrets
for wasted yesterdays.
You'd understand how hard I tried
to live on holy ground —
you'd see the shame within my heart
for times I let you down
But though you cannot view my heart
nor sense just what I feel,
I pray that you will never doubt
my love for you is real.
I'm asking God to guide you —
to fill you with His grace...
to grant you mercy, peace, and joy...
and all your fears erase;
to give you faith to trust in Him...
to wrap you in his love;
to hold you safe within His arms...
and bless you from above.

It doesn't matter that you're grown,
we're never far apart —
because forevermore, my child,
I'll hold you in my heart!

Magic Words

"I was wrong" and "I'm sorry" —
"I'll listen to you;"
"Forgive me"..."You're special"
"What shall we do?"

"I'll help you"..."Please"..."Thank you" —
"No problem"..."You're right" —
How could such phrases
set problems aright?

Yet real power they hold
when spoken in love
from a heart that's controlled
by the Father above.

Such "magic words"
bring hope to the soul;
they'll mend broken hearts
and make relationships whole.

With problems acknowledged
and forgiveness applied —
our love will grow stronger
as we walk side by side.

My Love

How can I say what I feel in my heart?
No words are sufficient, My Love.
I know without doubt you were placed in my life
as a gift from our Father above.
At a time when I felt overwhelmed and distressed
and thought I must face life alone,
you helped me to dream of the future again
with confidence I'd never know.
I've learned I can trust you, and give you my word
that to you I'll be faithful and true;
I've no fear of the pathway or what waits ahead
because I will face it with you.
I promise to love you through laughter and tears,
to listen when you need my ear;
I'll not doubt you but pledge my respect and support
so betrayal you need never fear.
We will dance in the rain, and walk on the beach —
hold hands and giggle like kids...
drink chocolate milkshakes, sled in the snow,
and welcome our future grandkids!
Hand-in-hand, heart-to-heart, we'll live every day
as together we'll weather life's storms;
we'll celebrate vict'ries and through every trial
find solace in each other's arms.
Now I thank you, My Darling, for all that you are,
you're truly the love of my life;
and with God's help I'll show you in all that I do
I'm proud to be known as your wife!

No Longer a Child

I think back over the years and can't believe how they've flown.
You're no longer a child, and the love that binds us has
grown stronger with time.
Until I held you, I didn't understand what motherhood meant.
At that moment my life changed forever.
Realities and emotions that I'd never before experienced
took me by surprise.
I recall how my heart almost burst with wonder at the
way God designed you,
and the delight I found in touching your tiny fingers and toes.
You're a miracle!
I wonder at your unique personality; because of you I know
that human life is priceless.
I've discovered the joy that comes from giving to someone with
no thought of receiving,
and am filled with the desire to give you more.
Yes, motherhood changed me.
I've felt exhilaration at the sunshine of your smile,
and my heart has been crushed by your tears.
I've been held captive by the fear that I wouldn't "do it right,"
and that you would bear scars from my mistakes —
but, by the grace of God, we've both survived, and amazingly
are able to accept and forgive each other's limitations.
My horizons have broadened as I've experienced the
world from your perspective,
and I marvel at the lessons you've taught me.
Although I've been frequently possessed by the fierce desire
to protect you from pain,
I've come to realize that sometimes the very pain I've tried to avoid has
been an instrument that has helped carve the capacity
for compassion and empathy
into both of our hearts. Often hurts have fashioned enduring strength on
the anvil of perseverance.
I pray you'll forgive me for the times I've failed you and that you'll know
I've always tried to do what I believed to be best for you.

One of the most difficult things I've ever done is to set you
free to make your
own choices. You've learned valuable lessons and I know that,
with God's help,
you can face whatever life hands you. You haven't
let difficulties destroy your
faith, nor cause you to "give up." I am so very proud of you!
Shared joys and griefs, celebrations and disappointments
as well as the challenges
of day to day living have all served to link our hearts with respect,
acceptance,
and hope.
No, nothing has been the same since you were born —
On that day I became a wealthy woman because I began
to learn my heart's
capacity for love --- a love of the kind that is unique to
a mother and her child.
I'm so thankful God gave me the special privilege of being
part of your life!
I love you,
Mom

Open Arms

I wake in the dark hours of the night with a heavy heart.
I wonder where you are
and what you are doing.
Are you okay?
I weep.
I long to have you near —
to hear your voice and to hold you
to know that you are safe.
I don't understand your choices,
How I wish I could make you see what you're doing to yourself
and to those that love you!
You have so much potential for a bright future,
but you're throwing it away;
you seem to be on the road to self-destruction.
If I could make the right choices for you,
I would —
but, of course, I can't.
I pray your eyes will be opened to the possible consequences of your
actions —
consequences that will almost certainly lead to heartbreak,
disaster, and ruined lives.
Looking back in time, maybe there were times I let you down,
but I never meant to.
Please forgive me and remember that
I love you —
NOTHING can ever change that.
AND, because I love you, I beg of you
to surrender completely to the One who loves you far more
than our feeble minds can comprehend —
the One who gave His life for you —
The One who will never desert nor disappoint you — NOT EVER!
I pray you will place your life in His hands;

you'll find that He is able to make of you
more than you could possibly imagine.
He will guide you to make the right choices.
When you come to know Him as I do,
You'll love Him, too —
and you'll discover that life will take on new meaning.
I've spoken to Him many times on your behalf
and although I can't always be with you
He can — if you'll trust Him.
He and I both wait with open arms for you, Dear One,
with open arms of love.

Sweet Dreams

I stand at your bedside and watch you sleep,
your frail body a shadow of who you used to be.
I wonder where you are....
are you dreaming of happy days gone by
or are you looking through the windows of Heaven?
Do you understand the realities of your present situation?
I hesitate to wake you, to speak your name; will you know who I am?
Will I be calling you back into a world of pain and harsh reality?
You're trapped inside a body that has grown too tired and
weak to function —
you would never have chosen this — but it wasn't your call.
Through the years you've been fiercely independent,
never complaining...nurturing those around you —
especially your children.
You've been our inspiration, our strength, our confidante,
the one who's always made us feel special.
You've taught us to be strong by being our example.
Oh, how I wish for one more day to spend with you —
a day when your mind and body would be able to function
as they once did.
I would tell you how thankful I am for you —
how very proud I've always been of you —
how blessed I am that you're my mom.
Thinking back over the years, I realize you made many sacrifices for me,
and you never made a big deal out of them;
you simply did whatever it took to make things as wonderful as possible
for me.
Not one time have I ever doubted your love —
for it was demonstrated clearly through your every word, touch, and deed.
At the time I didn't realize what an extraordinary mother you were —
but I do now.
Yet, as I stand here and watch you

I struggle to hold back the tears;
how I wish it were possible to "fix" things for you —
to "make it all better" like you have done so many times
through the years for me
...but it isn't possible
and I know it.
I hurt for you
and pray that God will bring you relief and release
from your suffering and state of dependence...
I don't understand why you are having to endure this existence — for it
isn't really living — but I know that God makes no mistakes so I must
trust Him to do what is
best for you.
In my heart, I know He will grant you peace, honor, and a restoration of
your
dignity —
if not in this life,
then the next.
Sweet dreams today and every day —
'til you awake with a perfect mind and body in your brand-new
Heavenly home!
I'll see you there. I love you.

Pathway

When someone who tries to oppose me
and seems to hold the upper hand,
life feels unfair and hurtful
because of his selfish demands.
I'm prone to fight back and get even
to form a cruel plan of attack —
and use hateful words as weapons
but a Voice from within holds me back:

"Child, this treatment you're getting's not pleasant
but here's what I want you to do —
respond with respect and submission
as I set the example for you.
When my foes betrayed and assaulted,
I prayed and forgave them their sin;
now I've placed you here with this person
that My love through your life may touch him."

As I ponder the truth of this message,
I know I need help in the task,
and I find in the scripture the promise
that all I need do is to ask.
For each action against me is measured
by my Father who plans it for good;
so I'll trust Him to make my behavior
honor His name as it should.
Then at times when I feel like a doormat
upon which my enemy trods...
instead I'll become a pathway
that will lead this person to God.

What Mothers Do

Do you daily do the laundry
and clean smudges from the wall...
wash the dishes, scrub the floors
and seek bargains at the mall?
Are you nurse and cook and chauffeur,
teacher, counselor, referee?
Is your schedule overloaded
so one moment's never free?
Do your loved ones take for granted
that their needs will all be met?
Has your family finished eating —
but you've not started yet?
Does bedtime often come and go
but there's no rest for you?
Do you long for conversation —
but no one has a clue?
Would you sometimes like to run away
for just a little while?
Have you often been bewildered
by the questions of a child?
Do you daily turn to God in prayer
when answers you don't know?
Is your refuge in the Father's arms
when there's nowhere else to go?
Then it sounds like you're quite normal
and the thing that's best for you
is simply keep on "keepin' on" —
for that's what Mothers do!

Will You Love Me?

I wonder what you see when you look at me.
I know that my hair style and clothing are very different than yours;
I try to be like my friends, so I'll blend in —
I don't like to be different because, the truth is,
often I'm very unsure of myself.
I don't want to be laughed at or thought "un-cool."
Growing up is hard to do — in fact,
it's plain scary at times and I often feel alone.
I'm not an adult yet, but neither am I a child —
frankly, I don't really know who I am, or what's expected of me...
but I'm trying hard to find out.
People ask me what I want to be when I "grow up" —
and I panic because I don't know.
The future looks pretty scary:
I go to school and wonder if someone will come into my
classroom and destroy us all...
or if terrorists will blow us off the map.
Has there ever been a time like this in the history of the world?
I hear people talk about how bad the economy is,
I see family break-ups, and I read in the news
headlines of tragedy after tragedy.
Is there any hope?
How I long to talk to someone who will really listen to me —
someone who will take the time to hear,
not just my words, but what I'm really trying to say...
someone who will reassure me that this Jesus
I've heard about is truly reliable —
someone who will be a true reflection of Him
and someone who is willing to show me by example how to live for Him.
I look at you and wonder if you might be that person,
but I don't know how to approach you or what to say;
I'm afraid that you'll think I'm not very smart...

or maybe that I'm "weird" because of all these thoughts I have...
or worse, maybe you'd think I was wasting your time.
Although I'm much younger than you,
I have feelings and I don't want to be hurt.
I'm afraid you might turn me away because you may not understand
how much I need you in my life.
I desperately want to know that I matter to someone, is that someone you?
If you have the time and are willing to take a chance on me,
we could be really good friends.
I would love to be part of your life — to know you and have you know me.
I wonder how you looked and felt at my age:
Did you feel alone and confused? Were you afraid?
Did your future look scary?
Will you share with me some of the things you've learned about life?
Can we go for a walk or make cookies together?
Can I help you wash your car or rake your leaves?
I just want to know that you enjoy my company —
that you see me as important to you...
I already know that you're important to me.
With God's help, we can help each other get through life's challenges —
and because we're together, the journey will not be as difficult!
Are you willing to take the risk of getting to know me
and letting me know you?
Will you love me and pray for me?
Do you believe that I'm worth spending time with?
Dear Senior Saint, please say "Yes." I'm waiting!

You'll Come to Me

"Call me if you need me,"
you say with good intent —
but do you really want to help —
if so, to what extent?
Will you visit when I'm lonely
and sit close by my side?
Can I trust you'll keep my secret thoughts
if in you I should confide?
Can I count on you to understand
when words are hard to say? —
and if, as friends, we disagree
will you love me anyway?
Will you set me free to be myself
and not my faults reveal?
Do you care enough to listen
if I tell you how I feel?
If "yes" to these you answer,
then what I need you'll see —
and I won't have to call you...
but you will come to me.

Spiritual Lessons

Empty Egg

A little plastic Easter egg
today was handed me;
expecting that it hid a prize
I opened it to see.

But much to my astonishment
not a thing it held —
just empty space surrounded by
a hard, synthetic shell.

Disappointment pricked my heart,
my lips curled in a frown;
this symbol of the Easter time
had really let me down!

Then suddenly I saw the truth
that banished my despair;
Jesus' tomb is vacant —
death couldn't hold Him there!

So now this egg will be for me
a symbol of Christ's grave —
abandoned when my Lord arose
in power my soul to save!

Forgiveness

Temptation softly called my name;
I yielded to its charm.
I kept it hidden from man's view
and didn't see its harm.
But every wicked thought I had —
each act, intent, and deed
that I'd concealed so carefully
quite clearly God could see.
Convicted for my evil ways
I turned to God in prayer —
confessed my sin and claimed His grace
then found forgiveness there!

Free!

The hurt that consumed me was vicious and deep —
I'd been wronged, betrayed, and maligned;
I couldn't let go of the anger I felt —
revenge and ill will filled my mind.
As I counted injustices done unto me
my heart grew heavy with hate;
I tried to decide how to "settle the score"
and how to retaliate.
Then I was reminded of what Jesus said —
"Remember that vengeance is Mine:
love those who've wronged you and fully forgive
that your light in the darkness will shine."
I handed my burden of hatred to Christ
and prayed for the grace to forgive;
He flooded my heart with mercy and love
now free from hate's bondage I live.

God Knows

We listen as the organ plays
and sing in one accord;
we bow our heads as if in prayer...
and say we love the Lord.
We place within the offering plate
our gifts to help the poor;
we hear the preacher tell us how
God's word is true and sure.
Yet all the while we're thinking of
somewhere we'd rather be...
and making plans for what we'll do
and who we're going to see.
We think that just by showing up
we're doing what we should...
but our hearts are full of self and sin —
not of God and good.
The image that we daily show
may fool our friends and foes —
but what and who we really are —
rest assured that God knows!

God's Ways

I stand in awe at the workings of God;
His ways are quite different than mine.
Nothing can happen that He doesn't know;
He draws the master design.
What I view as tragic, He plans for good —
His grace every moment I claim;
in each of my trials, He provides faith —
from what appears loss He brings gain.
Sometimes when I think I've come to the end
He shows me I've only begun—
and when all of my strength is vanished away
He helps me the race to run.
God's my Hope when life's hopeless; my Light when all's dark;
my Peace in the midst of life's storms...
and tho' I can't fathom His methods and ways
I know that I'm safe in His arms!

Grace Alone

I tried my best to earn God's love
and set my mind at ease;
I thought that surely doing good
would fill my soul with peace.
I gave my offerings to the poor,
made sure my tithes were paid;
visited the sick and frail —
no confidence betrayed.
I taught a class in Bible school —
invited folks to church,
sang songs each Sunday in the choir
and in God's word I searched.
To every task I gave my all
and tried to do it right —
yet all my earnest efforts failed
as I wearied of the fight.
With desperate plea, I cried, "Oh, God,
help me, I'm Your own!"
In a still small voice I heard Him say,
"You're mine by grace alone.
No work can bring you peace and joy
to fill your empty soul;
rest in Me and what I've done —
then you'll be truly whole!"

If Not I

I pray someone will teach my child
of Jesus and His love;
I hope someone will lead my friends
to that heav'nly home above.
Some person ought to feed the poor
and help the weak to walk —
and there's a need with lonely folks
to simply sit and talk.
Somebody should in distant lands
share salvation's plan
and give great offerings faithfully
to care for hurting man.
Someone ought to welcome those
who're strangers in our midst —
and surely one must visit those
who're grieving o'er lost kids.
Deep within my heart I ask —
to meet these needs, who'll try?
Who will claim these needful tasks —
who'll do them — if not I?

It's Amazing

Sometimes by life I'm overwhelmed
and feel I can't go on;
circumstances shout at me —
"Give up! All hope is gone!"
Despair says, "Things are really bad!"
Fear taunts, "Don't you try!"
"What's the point? — just call it quits,"
I hear Depression cry.
But deep within my heart I sense
a Voice speak tenderly;
"I love you, Child, this battle's mine,
depend in full on Me.
"Recall the trials you've faced before —
you've safely made it through;
and when you couldn't help yourself
I even carried you.
"Now give Me all your doubts and fears —
place your eyes on ME;
peace and joy I'll give to you —
I've won the victory!
"I'm always working for your good —
through trials and tests and strife —
and when your tasks on earth are through
you have eternal life!
"Before Me you will bow in awe —
your heart in worship praising —
and say of all I've done for you —
'Lord, it IS amazing!'"

Life on the Mountain

Up to the top of the mountain
went James, and Peter, and John
and there transfigured before them
Jesus' face shone bright like the sun.
They wanted to stay on the mountain
but God's perfect plan had been made;
the cross lay in wait for the Savior
where the cost of man's sin would be paid.
Like Peter, I long for the mountain —
not the vales of life and its cares —
yet in the chasm of heartbreak
I find the power of prayer.
Though I still dream of life on the mountain
where free from all problems I'd be,
there are lessons to learn in the valleys
that God's planned especially for me!
Wherever He leads, I will trust Him;
my vision is fixed on His face —
and even in life's deepest valleys,
I dwell in His bountiful grace.

Life's a Journey

Life's journey has its twists and turns —
up mountains and through vales;
sometimes it leads o'er desert sands...
at times o'er ocean swells.

Some paths allow companionship
as hand-in-hand friends walk;
others must be trod alone
where toughest truths are taught.

The route at times grows rough and long —
fierce storms with thunder roll;
detours loom and dangers rise
that test man's heart and soul.

But when the way grows treacherous
and I grow tired and worn
I'll travel on, trust God and pray
my strength may be reborn.

For I can know whate'er life's road
it's planned by God above —
then I'm assured He walks with me
and guides me in His love!

Lifesaver

I sometimes speak a kindly word
and often share a smile
and many times, I hold a hand
and sit and talk awhile.
And tho' these things have good intent,
they all fall short indeed
each time I fail to share with folks
the One they really need.
I cannot tarry with the news
of God's salvation plan —
the message of His love and grace
through Christ for sinful man.
I'll ask the Lord to fashion me
into a real "life-saver" —
by making me a messenger
who'll lead souls to my Savior!

Link in a Chain

Some noble deed I'd hoped I could do —
a grandiose scheme, impressive and new —
a marvelous plan I'd announce to the world
proclaiming real peace under banners unfurled.
But day after day and year after year
no feat of great triumph to me became clear.

Yet oft' at my whisper, a tiny babe smiles
and stories I read encourage a child;
soup from my kitchen nourishes kin —
and words that I speak comfort a friend.
Coins from my pocket for the homeless buy shoes
and a note that I write carries good news.

With God's help I see that meeting a need,
like a link in a chain is vital indeed.
It's not just the triumphs of gigantic size
that count as success in His loving eyes —
It's each faithful effort done in His name
with not a desire for earthly acclaim.

So I can take heart in the smallest of things
and trust that true blessings to others they'll bring.
Each day I'll move forward, God's hand holding mine,
changing the world one deed at a time;
for what I once questioned, I now understand —
each link in life's chain is part of God's plan!

Made Complete

I sought success in earthly things
but found within my heart
that wealth and accolades I won
did not real joy impart.
For every time I tried and reached
a new and temporal goal,
there still remained an emptiness
inside my yearning soul.
I prayed that God would change my life,
and searched His holy word
then from its pages as I read
the truth to me occurred —
Like filthy rags my own attempts
would prove to be but vain;
an empty heart cannot be filled
by fame or earthly gain.
I'm made complete by Jesus Christ
when truly Him I seek —
it's not my deeds, but trusting Him
that fills my heart with peace!

Much More

I prayed for an answer, but got no reply,
and disheartened and doubtful I grew;
if I simply tried harder to live for the Lord
I thought what I asked, He would do.
But days turned to months, and months into years —
I begged God to answer this prayer;
tears wet my cheeks and doubts plagued my heart
and I began my descent to despair.
Why didn't God answer? Was I out of His will?
From such questions I could not refrain.
Was there something I'd missed that I needed to do?
Was all of my waiting in vain?
He asked that I trust and stay faithful to Him
when completely hopeless my view;
for in His great wisdom He knew the right time
that His answer my faith would renew.
But then it arrived — when I'd given up —
when impossible seemed what I'd asked;
but praise the dear Lord, He'd planned all along
to do this miraculous task.
Then I saw clearly God loves me so much
He'd carefully planned from the start
to teach me to trust Him, for in His own time
He'd accomplished His will in my heart!
Now looking back after all of these years
when I've seen this prayer answered at last...
the truth is apparent — I'm truly amazed —
God gave me much more than I'd asked!

My Worth

I'm judged every day by the folks that I meet
by the way that I look, or I act,
they view as essential the things I possess
or condemn me if any I lack.
They count it important my gender and age
my weight, and my color of hair —
the place that I live, the car that I drive —
my wealth, and the clothes that I wear.
They see my flesh, not my heart nor my thoughts,
and they think my intelligence key;
of import's my talent, the job that I hold,
yet they care not a bit about ME.
But God views my soul with mercy and grace
and to Him I'm of infinite worth;
His message of love was sent in His Son
when as a human He came to earth!
My value was settled on Calvary's hill
and the tomb in which Jesus laid;
for when He came forth, Death was destroyed
and sin's price in full He had paid!
There'll soon come a time when He'll bid me come Home;
and Heaven's beauty and wealth I'll explore;
there I'll dwell as a child of the King with my Lord
and my worth will be questioned no more!

On Him

Tapers glow in candelabra;
ornate urns hold fresh bouquets.
Anxious guests await her entry;
nuptial organ music plays.
Then the bride steps through the portal —
dressed in gown of regal style;
all eyes marvel at her beauty,
her face aglow with radiant smile.
Bridesmaids watch with handsome groomsmen
as the wedding march begins,
but as the bride moves toward her bridegroom —
her vision's fixed on him!
With tenderness they speak their vows,
their marriage to begin;
most folks still are watching HER —
but she sees only HIM.
The preacher says they're man and wife;
excitement fills the room...
and as the congregation watches
the bride smiles at her groom.
I can't help but think of Jesus
Who awaits the church, His bride;
in her march to meet her Bridegroom
does her sight on Him Abide?
Someday soon I'll enter Heaven
where a mansion's built for me;
tho' its beauty is astounding,
it's my Lord I want to see.
For I know my Savior's waiting
and He'll bid me come on in;
all its wonders won't distract me —
for my eyes will be on Him!

Pearls

Grains of sand in an oyster's shell
constantly prod and annoy —
but the delicate mollusk makes of them pearls
that exemplify beauty and joy.
I pray God will use every trial of my life
to fashion me as a fine gem —
that always quite clearly, without any doubt
will honor and glorify Him!

Peter and Me

Peter's hopes had collapsed when Jesus had died,
so he went back to his nets by the sea;
ignoring his call as a fisher of men —
what Jesus intended him be.
After fishing all night, six friends by his side,
their efforts proved futile and vain;
but a Voice from the shore said, "Recast on the right,"
and a bounteous harvest they claimed.
When Peter saw it was Jesus, he jumped from the boat
and to the Master did swim;
back on the shore, "Do you love Me?" he heard —
three times Jesus asked this of him.
"Yes, Lord, You know that I love You!" he cried
then was told to care for Christ's sheep;
'twas clear Christ forgave his failures and faults —
and that he had a mission to keep.
Like Peter, I face disappointments and trials
and I'm tempted by sinful old ways
but my Savior forgives and whispers to me
there are tasks I'm to do every day.
By God's grace I will do each thing that He asks
so His love in my life all may see.
For He forgives and equips His frail children to serve —
even those like Peter and me!

Sleepless Nights

Once again, I find myself enduring a long and sleepless night.

Sleep evades me, though I'm exhausted.
    My body seems at war with my spirit
        and the hours of darkness crawl by, minute by minute.
            I long for rest, for escape from weariness, and for renewal —
                but they seem destined not to be.
    Aches and pains beset my body —
        dilemmas plague my thoughts —
            and concerns bruise my heart.

Lord, I don't understand.
    What lessons do I need to learn?
        Am I doing something wrong?
            Have I wandered out of Your will?
                How much longer will this desert in my life last?
There've been other times when I've felt bewildered —
    but never a time quite like this...when the future seems a vapor
    with no way it can be provoked into substance.
The props are gone — those "securities" that falsely assured me that things
    were okay —
        that all was "normal."
But now I think I'm beginning to realize that You would have me place
    ALL my trust
        in YOU ALONE...
           with no external "props" on which to depend.

Lord,
    I ask for grace to do this, because in myself I can do nothing of lasting
        value.
    Help me set my sights ON and IN You. Please give me the faith to obey
        You

and to trust that You ARE accomplishing Your purposes.
Grant that during this sleepless night,
    I will come to know You better,
        love You more deeply,
            and to trust You completely...
    and that at its end
        I will praise You
for staying with me through the dark hours...
        for holding me close...
            and for assuring me
                of
            Your glorious presence.
I will thank You for this sleepless night and see it as a time
        when You are equipping me
            with Your wisdom and strength
                to face whatever.

Blame

I pointed at my mom and dad —
my spouse, my kids, the friends I had
and placed the blame for wrongs I'd done
upon the shoulders of each one...
but in God's word, I now can see —
the guilty one is really
— Me!

The Dream

I dreamed I stood at Heaven's gate
my earthly life at end;
but there an angel asked me
why I should enter in.
With confidence I smiled and said,
"Why that's not hard at all!
Just listen, and of things I've done,
you'll surely stand in awe.
"I went to church 'most every week —
placed offerings in the plate;
sang hymns and taught a Bible class
and no one did I hate.
"Each Christmas I helped feed the poor —
the smiles I wore spread cheer...
and when my neighbor needed aid
I quickly volunteered."
The angel sadly shook his head,
"You've lived your life in vain;
your works are but as filthy rags —
by sin your heart is stained.
"You never turned to Jesus Christ
forgiveness to receive;
you turned your back on Calvary —
I'm sorry —
you must leave."

The Silence

God, I'm desperate;
I cry out to You
but hear no response.
The Silence baffles me.
Am I where I'm supposed to be —
or have I drifted out of Your will?
What am I supposed to do?
It seems all my "securities" are crumbling
around me.
There's nothing left to trust
but You.
I know that You're enough
so why do I doubt?
Forgive me: rescue me —
I can't help myself.
I'm weak.
Only You know that I'm living in a state of perpetual panic;
I know this isn't what You want for me —
give me faith to trust You.
Even though I don't see evidence of what You're doing in my life
I know You have a plan.
You never fail.
You've promised You'll never forsake Your child;
I'm Yours
so though I don't feel Your presence,
You are with me.
Thank You.
In the silence I'll trust You
and when You see fit
the Silence will end
and I'll understand.
I'll wait where You have placed me;

help me find peace
and Your purpose
and help me remember
that sometimes
life's most meaningful lessons
can only be learned
in the Silence.

The Well

The Samaritan woman drank from life's cup
of pleasure that tainted her name;
seeking relief from a thirst never quenched
she tasted frustration and shame.
But Jesus was waiting one day by the well
where she sought her bucket to fill;
as she drank of the Water He offered she found
relief from her thirst sure and real.
I, too, was searching for respite and balm
from thirsts raging out of control —
and naught that the world had to offer could quench
the longing down deep in my soul.
But Jesus stood ready to heal my poor heart
parched by sin's desert waste
with Water abundant, alive, without end —
supplied by His unbounded grace!
So, I drank from The Well and was changed by His love
for full pardon and mercy He gives;
He's the Answer I longed for, the end of my search
and forever within me He lives!

Unique

No matter how hard I try
I don't fit in;
I feel different.
I long to be understood
and accepted as I am
but people seem suspicious
of my motives.
I wonder why they can't see
that I'm who I seem to be...
with no hidden agenda.
I don't like games of pretense.
People matter to me;
I really care
and long to know
that someone really cares
about me —
not for what I can do,
nor for what I have —
but for who I am...
and yet when I stop to think
I realize —
Jesus
is that Someone
Who knows me,
loves me and accepts me
and He is the Someone
who made me and each of His children
different and unique.

Victory Cry

I walked in the garden, alone and confused,
overcome by grief and despair,
with no inkling at all how my life would be changed
by the lesson that waited there.
I spied what appeared but a lowly worm
entombed in its fragile shroud,
but this crypt would equip it with beautiful wings
to soar through the sky and the clouds.
Then to my memory came Calvary's cross
and the way Death thought it had won,
When Christ said, "It's finished!" and went to the grave
Satan thought he'd destroyed God's own Son!
So I'll try to remember when problems prevail,
and I'm tempted to question "Lord, why?" —
what seems like "the end" is really a "womb"
where God's making a butterfly!
When this life is over and God welcomes me home,
only then will I understand why
earth's trials were needed in His masterful plan —
and "It's finished!" in vict'ry I'll cry!

Waiting Time

Lord, I sit and wait not knowing
what the future holds for me,
but I believe You know what's best
and all's controlled by Thee.
I'm struggling with uncertainty
and bow beneath its load —
I've never faced a thing like this
nor walked so rough a road.
As troubling thoughts assault my mind,
fears invade my soul;
waiting time is difficult
and out of my control.
So clear my heart from disarray
and make my will as Thine;
show to others through my life
your grace and love divine.
Please give me faith to trust in You
though Your purpose I can't see...
and I'll give thanks that through this time
You're waiting here with me!

What If?

Sometimes I awake heart heavy with care
afraid of what's waiting ahead;
in need of the courage to face a new day
"What ifs" — fill me with dread.
"What if" — friends desert me? "what if" — I'm alone?
"What if" — in bereavement I cry?
"What if" — I look foolish or am misunderstood?
"What if" — my dreams crumble and die?
"What if" — I'm attacked, maligned, or betrayed?
"What if" — in my tasks I should fail?
"What if" all possessions and health I would lose?
"What if" — disaster prevails?
Then it seems I can hear, from deep in my heart,
a Voice speaks softly to me;
"Dear one I've some questions; now listen and see
just what your answers will be —
WHAT IF you'd not worry? WHAT IF you'd not fret?
WHAT IF from gloom you'd refrain?
WHAT IF you would trust Me to know what is best?
WHAT IF you'd not fuss nor complain?
WHAT IF you would praise Me? WHAT IF you'd give thanks?
WHAT IF you would seek Me in prayer?
WHAT IF in your trials you'd rely on My word —
you'd find there's no need for despair.
For I'm you Defender, Redeemer, and Guide,
your Savior, your Father, your Friend,
My grace will not fail you; you don't walk alone;
on My love you can fully depend.
Now give Me your cares; the battle's been won;
I'll equip you for life's every task;
and when you're in need of My wisdom and strength,
all you need do, Child, is ask!

What's Waiting Ahead

When life proves a challenge and I feel confused
my heart's encumbered with dread;
but I am assured by truths in God's word
He knows what's waiting ahead.

Jesus went to the cross on Calvary's hill
where He willingly suffered and bled —
paid for my sin with His life for He knew
that victory waited ahead.

Tho' my friends think me foolish and question my deeds
I'll not doubt, but trust God instead;
I'll go where He leads with a peace in my heart —
He's with me, whatever's ahead.

I'll obey Him each day tho' I don't understand
and claim all the truths that he said —
for the trials of this life pale when compared
to the glory of what's waiting ahead!

What I'll Leave Behind

No matter where I enter in
folks have gone before —
and evidence of who was there
I see inside the door.
For in each place in every room
so clearly are the signs
of what folks thought important —
by what they've left behind.
Family photos on the shelf
of special moments shared
reveal the love and pride folks felt —
for whom they really cared.
The atmosphere in every home
though palace or a shack —
if filled with lack of care repels —
but faith and love attract.
This sets my mind to wondering
what folks will learn of me
by what I'll leave behind when I
on Earth do cease to be.
Will they see that love and peace
filled my heart and soul?
Will evidence that at all times
Christ my life controlled?
Will they see that smiles or frowns
monopolized my life?
Will they recall that joy I shared —
or stirred up stress and strife?
Will wisdom in the way I lived
show clearly when I'm gone?
Will my earthly life have mattered
to the folks who must go on?

I pray that what I leave behind will speak
with voice so crystal clear —
that folks will never question
that 'twas them I held so dear!

Why Are We Fighting?

What are we thinking, dear brothers —
   why are we fighting this way?
Let's stop and think what we're doing
   and see who we're hurting today.
Children are watching and listening —
   our youth, confused by our deeds;
a lost world is looking in horror
   as we sow disharmony's seeds.
Let's realize our enemy's Satan —
   he laughs with glee as we fight;
we're supposed to love one another
and in darkness shine forth as The Light.
Instead, we act like opponents
   whose goal is to injure and kill —
forgetting that we are God's children —
   ignoring our dear Father's will.
So, let's stop fighting each other
   and ask God to cleanse us from sin,
renew our love for each other
   and in triumph o'er Satan we'll win!

Special Occasions

Beside the Christmas Tree

Lights and tinsel, bells and bows,
carols in the air —
reindeer perched on chimney tops,
angels everywhere;
fancy trees and wreaths of green,
presents wrapped in red,
singing, laughter, shopping trips,
hot chocolate, gingerbread...
but this Yuletide I don't know
just what I'm going to do;
how can I survive the pain
of Christmas without you?
For all that's left are photographs
made of you and me —
festive scenes of holidays
beside the Christmas tree.
Yet I'm sure you're well and happy,
and I like to think it's true
that you somehow know how very much
I loved and treasured you.
For you're celebrating Christmas now
in Heaven's perfect land
where everything your heart desires
you hold at your command.
I'll someday join you in that place
of ever-sunny skies
where every day's a holiday
and there'll be no more "good-byes."
But until then within my heart
I'll hold you close to me
and pray that God will fill the void
beside the Christmas tree.

Christmas Rush

With Yuletide fast approaching
I had no time to waste;
with everything that must be done
I had to move with haste.
I rushed out to the nearest mall,
went on a shopping spree,
wrapped three dozen presents
and placed them 'neath the tree.
Next I cleaned and dusted
in case some friends dropped by;
mailed a hundred greeting cards,
and baked a mincemeat pie.
I hung the Christmas stockings,
stuffed a ten-pound bird;
read the Christmas play again
rehearsing every word.
I raced to choir practice —
got home just after ten;
folded laundry, hemmed a skirt,
then dozed off in the den.
'Twas then I heard my Savior speak,
"Child, what's this all about?
you say that it's My birthday —
and yet you've left Me out.
"Today I waited patiently
to hear your voice in prayer,
but not one time My name you called —
you hurt Me; don't you care?
"My name you are dishonoring
for dear one, stop to see —
amidst this frantic 'Christmas' rush
that you've forgotten Me!"

One Perfect Gift

If I could give you a Christmas gift
it wouldn't be wrapped in bows —
but it would be the Gift of all gifts
that the true Christmas Spirit you'd know.
He'd wrap you securely in His perfect love —
in your soul fullest joy He'd release;
you'd have the assurance that He's in control
and your heart would be filled with His peace.
This Gift would abide forever with you
and guide you just where you should go;
He'd show you the things that matter in life
and help you God's truths to know.
This Gift is my Jesus, Who came as a babe
years ago to Bethlehem's stall ...
and lived as a man who died on a cross
where your debt and mine, He paid all.
So this Christmas season, I pray that you'll pause
and allow Him your burdens to lift —
for you'll never regret that you opened your heart
and accepted this One Perfect Gift.

God Sent You

God sends special people into our lives
at special times
to meet special needs —
those who have the rare ability
not only to do what must be done,
but who take us by surprise
because they go above and beyond the call of duty.
They are those who really care and aren't afraid to show it —
those who are equipped by God to do the seemingly impossible
in difficult circumstances
and yet perform the most menial task
as a labor of love.
You are one of those special people.
In one of the darkest hours of my life
God sent you to me.
In your eyes. I saw His compassion;
in your voice, I heard His concern;
and, in your touch, I felt His love.
You gave me strength and courage
to face the unthinkable —
and in your dedication
I found hope.
I will be forever grateful that you risked caring for me,
and by so doing,
built a bridge to my soul.
I can't forget that you cried with me —
and I knew you understood,
This brought me comfort.
Through you God has taught me that He really can bring good
from unspeakable pain.
Thank you for being a special person —
for caring about me

and for sharing the gift of yourself with me.
Please know that you've made a difference in my life
and that I'll always carry a part of you with me...
I wear your fingerprints on my heart.
You proved yourself a special person
in a special time of life —
one that God used to help bring healing to my broken heart.
Keep doing the same for others who come your way.
May God bless your every effort!

Souls and Stockings

On the outside all looks pretty;
folks seem to be just fine.
Their homes are decked in green and red
and smell of fragrant pine.
Underneath their Christmas trees
gift-wrapped presents lay,
while stockings hang from mantle shelves
awaiting Christmas day.
Piped-in music sets the tone;
holly "decks the halls;"
"Season's Greetings" fill the air
and tinsel drapes the walls.
Yes, all appears to be just great,
but looks can sure deceive...
for many folks want only that
their hurts will be relieved.
Like stockings hanging on a shelf
their hearts are empty, too.
They try to fill their barren lives
with lots of things to do.
But earthly things can't fill the void
and desperation mounts —
for they don't know the birth of Christ
is what life's all about.
For Jesus Christ desires to fill
the empty souls of men —
to give a purpose to our lives,
our broken hearts to mend.
For willingly He came to Earth
as God's own baby boy
that He could fill our barren hearts
with His love, peace, and joy!

The Reason for the Season

Wreaths of green adorn the doors —
stockings hang from shelves;
tiny reindeer pilot sleighs
that hold red-suited elves.
Frantic shoppers fill their carts
with toys and gifts galore
while "Ho, Ho, Hos" and "Jingle Bells"
echo through the stores.
It's plain to see that once again
Christmas time is here;
but what we ought to celebrate
we've left behind, I fear.
Let's pause to really think about
the purpose of this season
it isn't Santa Claus or shopping sprees —
Christ's birthday is the reason!
God sent His only Son to Earth
from Heaven's throne above
in flesh born of a virgin girl
to show mankind His love.
Jesus bridged the gap to God
because man wasn't able ...
and He became God's Gift of Love —
a babe, born in a stable!

Mom of the Bride

The pages of time have turned much too fast
and now she's no longer a child.
Her wedding day's here and I stand by and watch
as love lights her face with a smile.
Scenes from her girlhood flash thought my mind
(so clearly the mem'ries prevail!)
of days filled with learning what life's all about...
and each has its story to tell —

Mud pies in summer...
first day of school...
giggles at bedtime
and bending the rules;
tending her dollies...
scrapes climbing trees...
band-aids attempting
to hide her skinned knees!
Hour-long phone calls...
the first time she drove...
crushes and heartbreaks...
her first "puppy-love;"
testing her feelings...
learning her strengths...
using her talents
and stretching great lengths;
ultimate effort...
reaching new goals...
savoring life
as each venture unfolds...

My heart's filled with love as I ponder these things —
for each special mem'ry thankfulness brings.
Not pining for past days, but looking ahead —
I see not a girl, but a woman instead.
Her dreams she's fulfilling, her mind is mature,
her spirit is sweet, and her faith is secure.
The time has arrived — she'll soon be a wife;
how privileged I am to share in her life!
Forgive my emotion, these musings, and pride;
you see, I'm entitled...
I'm the mom of the bride!

Mom of the Groom

I can hardly believe that he is now grown
for the days of his childhood so quickly have flown!
He stands at the altar and waits with a smile
as his dearly beloved walks down the aisle.
Today he's committing his love and his life
to this special woman he'll claim as his wife.
Emotions take over; my eyes fill with tears
as I picture quite clearly earlier years —

the first time I held him...brisk morning strolls...
sampling the "goody" from cake batter bowls;
playing with puppies...learning to share...
teasing and laughter...saying his prayers;
rompers to blue jeans...starting to school...
scrapes, fractures, bruises...crew-cuts and curls...
bike rides and sports cars..."discovering" girls;
facing tough challenges...trying new things...
struggling with heartache...testing his "wings;"
talks late at night...out on his own...
emails and phone calls...coming back home;
looking to God when dreams came undone...
waiting for love and meeting "the one" —

My attention is brought to the present once more;
I can't return to days gone before.
No longer a boy who holds to my hand
but standing before me I see a fine man!
Strong, handsome, thoughtful — responsible, too,
starting his marriage with hopes bright and new.

What an honor to raise him and help him to grow
but now to another I must let him go.
That I am proud, it's safe to presume —
I've earned the right;
I'm the mom of the groom!

Prayer and Praise

Designed by the Father

Designed by my Heavenly Father —
what an awesome thought!
He carefully planned each part of me
and then each detail wrought.
Each breath I breathe, He gives me —
each hurt I feel, He knows;
each need I have, He satisfies —
each place I walk, He goes.
He fills my heart with wonder
as I seek His blessed face;
His mercies are unending
and He covers me with grace.
I'll praise His name forever
and rejoice in that I know —
my Father has designed me
because He loves me so!

Comfort Zone

I long to burrow deep into my comfort zone...
to sink my roots into the familiar.
I don't like change
for it requires risk —
a relocation
into the unknown realm of my faith.
It forces me to grow...
and growth can be both difficult and scary...
Yet I know in my heart
that I'll never be able to stretch my branches toward Heaven
unless I'm willing to bury the seed of self-will
in the soil of faith.
I cannot bear fruit
unless I'm transplanted into the soil of the unfamiliar
away from my comfort zone —
out of the realm of sight.
I fear the loss of security
and yet
I know that the only real security
is found
in the hands of the Master Gardener
He places me where I need to be...
keeps me anchored
when I need to stay...
and transplants me
when I need new soil
that I might thrive
and bear fruit.

He will make of me a strong tree
whose roots are grounded in Him alone
and whose branches reach toward Heaven
bearing fruit which honors Him.
I pray for faith
that I'll be willing to move beyond
my comfort zone!

No Reason to Complain

I'm prone to feel sorry for myself and to complain about how
difficult life is.
How really humbled I am when I stop and think that...

Many people in the world will never know
the luxury of a heated home, carpeted floors, or automobiles.
They won't in their entire lives eat a well-balanced meal,
flush a toilet, nor flip a light switch.
They'll go to sleep without the comfort of a mattress,
endure harsh weather without benefit of shelter,
and suffer pain without even the relief that an aspirin can bring.
They'll never benefit from a pair of eyeglasses, a hearing aid, or braces;
they just accept limitations which could be easily remedied
if they'd been born elsewhere.
Many can't read a book, write a letter, nor even sign their own names.
Attending school, shopping in a grocery store, or visiting a museum
are not options.
They will never taste ice cream, sit in an upholstered chair,
nor hear a newscast.
Shoes are a luxury; a change of clothes, an extravagance.
They will never hear of the love of Jesus, sing a hymn, nor own a Bible.
If they could walk in my footsteps for one hour
they'd be amazed that I have so much
and yet act ungrateful.
They'd think me spoiled, wasteful, and extremely wealthy —
and by the standards of most people in this world
I am.
They'd wonder why I'm not busy about my Father's business,
sharing His blessings and praising Him.
They'd marvel that I could find anything about which to grumble —
and they'd be right,
I have no reason to complain
for I am blest!

Prayer for Children from a Broken Home

Please hold them in Your hand, Lord,
and guard their little hearts;
help them feel Your presence
and make the fear depart.
They've lived through many battles
and heard cruel, bitter words;
please let them know without a doubt
their precious prayers you've heard.
Protect their tender minds, God,
from Satan's awful lies;
help them see the truth and then
the Evil One despise.
I ask You'll mend their fractured hearts
and make them whole and new;
give them hope and faith to know
that they can count on You.
Tho'
broken is their earthly home —
secure is Heav'n above...
and let them know, without a doubt,
the surety of Your love!

Prayer for Help Today

Dear Lord, help me today.
Let me not be plagued by yesterday's failures
nor live in fear of what tomorrow may hold.
Help me to live fully each moment,
celebrating its joys,
counting its blessings,
learning its lessons,
and tasting its victories
— even those that sometimes seem to be defeats!
Help me put things in perspective...
seeing those things which really matter...
and putting aside those things which would hinder Your purpose for me.
Let me not become deterred by pettiness
— nor sidetracked by greed.
Let me not try to "get even" —
instead help me trust You to put all things right.
Help me respond in love to those who would desire to bring me harm,
and remind me that I may be the only Bible they "read."
Help me to forgive, that through my forgiveness others may see You.
Use me in any way You choose, and give me the faith to believe that
You truly are working all things together for my good.
Fill me with an attitude of thanksgiving for everything
that comes into my life, that I may honor You.
Give me courage to stand for what's right,
to speak against injustice,
and to defend the helpless.
Help me to say nothing
when speaking would dishonor You.
Make my motives pure, my dealings honest,
and my integrity sure.
Give me the grace to accept whatever You plan for me.

Order each step, control every thought, and guide all my actions.
Motivate me with honor.
Let there be no doubt when my life is viewed by others
that I belong to You.
Amen.

Prayer for My Grown Daughter

Dear Lord,
 I try not to worry as I go about my daily tasks,
  but the ache just never goes away.
 I wonder where she is and what she's doing;
  Is she okay?
 I long for the phone to ring...to hear her voice —
  but at the same time, I struggle for words
   that will bring her hope.
 As much as I'd like to, I can't fix things for her
  nor take away the hurt;
 I can't fight her battles nor make her decisions.
  Where have the years gone? Life was so much simpler
   when she was a child.
    She's a parent now,
     trying to be both mother and father.
      The task overwhelms her at times, but she tries so hard!
    She's exhausted from the effort, and she feels so alone.
 Help her to know that although she's been betrayed by others,
  You, Lord, are always faithful!
 Help her see past this valley she's in
  and realize that without valleys there are no mountain tops.
 Give her the vision to know that things WILL get better —
  that You WILL bring good from this...
   that You have a plan for her life...
    and that she is never out of Your care.
 Help her to trust You and to know the joy and peace
  that come from serving You.
 I know that You love her even more than I do,
  and I ask that You protect, encourage, and strengthen her.
 Help me to remember that she's in Your hands —
  and that's the safest place for her to be!
     Amen!

Thank You for the Thorns

Lord, You've blessed me most abundantly
with home and precious kin —
with food to eat and clothes to wear
and many special friends.
You've given me two ears to hear,
two eyes that I may see;
a heart set free from sin's cruel bonds
where You reside with me.
For all of these I thank You, Lord,
by them I am amazed ...
and for each of all the millions more
Your Holy Name I praise.
But today, I want to thank You
for the blessings I've received
that came disguised as burdens —
whose worth I could not see.
For like thorns that thrive in gardens
wherever roses grow —
I can't grasp their purpose
but the Master Gardener knows.
Now looking back o'er heartbreaks
that I still don't understand —
You carried me through each of them
protected by Your hand.
So, when life's trials hit me hard
and I grow tired and worn...
please help me to remember, Lord,
to thank You for the thorns.

Life Everlasting

The wealthy young ruler asked at Christ's feet,
"Good Master, what can I do
to gain life eternal? — the answer I need
so, I've brought my question to You."
Jesus said unto him, "There's none good but God,
why is it that you call Me 'good'?…
You've been taught the commandments that man's to obey
but their meaning, have you understood?
Don't defraud and don't steal; don't lie and don't kill;
keep your body moral and pure;
honor your parents, and I say to you,
sell your goods and give to the poor."
While in love Jesus watched, the man walked away —
from his "riches" he chose not to part.
Forsaking God's Son, he held to earth's wealth,
and walked away, heavy of heart.
How tragic he trusted the world's paltry goods
and rejected the Savior that day;
for in clinging to what couldn't last he gave up
real life that would not pass away!
"Dear Father, I pray I'll reject and deny
the fleeting and false for what's true;
for life everlasting You've promised to us
who have placed all our trust, Lord, in You!"

So It Matters

Lord, when I look at the world and its needs
my efforts to help seem quite small;
I wonder just how the things that I do
can make any difference at all.
My talents seem few, I've nothing to boast;
what good can one person do?
But all that I am and all that I have
I willingly give now to You.
Make of my life what You'd have me to be —
lead where You'd have me go;
equip me with power to serve in Your name
and use me Your mercies to show.
Help me bring comfort to those who have hurts
and laughter to souls who need cheer;
give through me courage to those who've lost hope
and promise where there has been fear.
Use my heart as Your chapel, my thoughts as Your own —
make my lips Your trumpet of praise;
fashion my life so it matters, Dear Lord,
that Your love will flow through me each day!

Not Ok

You ask me how I'm doing
and I tell you I'm okay.
But if I'd bare my heart to you
here is what I'd say:

"I'm not okay and there's no way
for you to understand;
no two lives are just the same
nor dealt an equal hand.
"You don't know just how I feel —
you can't know what I need!
Don't tell me what I ought to do
nor judge my words or deeds!
"The truth is I'm not who I was —
I've lost a part of me;
I don't know who 'I' really am
nor what I'm meant to be.
"I long for what I used to have
but know those days are gone;
mem'ries flood my heart with 'us'...
and I feel so alone.
"I find I'm in a world of 'pairs'
where I just don't fit in;
a wounded bird that's lost its song
I ache for hope again.
"So when I speak my loved one's name,
please let me reminisce;
hold my hand and let me cry —
a friend is made for this.

"And tho' right now I'm not okay
I pray my heart will mend;
from wisdom gained from loss and pain
I'll learn to live again."

The Long Good-bye

I smile as I think of times now gone by —
days when we laughed, and we played...
and cherish glad mem'ries of you and of me
in my heart forever displayed.

We served our dear Savior and studied His word
and worshipped with songs of praise;
together we knelt at the altar in faith
and with hearts full of love there we prayed.

But today I stand helpless as you fade away —
the one I have loved so long —
and pray on our journey of gradual good-byes
our Lord will Himself make me strong

For I often gaze deeply into your eyes
but am filled with sadness and dread
when I try to find there the essence of you —
and see a stranger instead.

You'd never have chosen to leave me this way
and I find I ask our Lord, "why?"
for this is the hardest thing I've ever done —
facing Earth's last, long good-bye.

But I wonder if you know that this is "good-bye"?
Are you feeling of "us" the loss?
Or in your mind's eye do you quite clearly see
God is bearing with us this cruel cross?

I'll cling to the truth God makes no mistakes
and never we'll part by and by...
for Heaven's made sweeter for you and for me
because of Earth's "long good-bye!"

Love

Love's not candy and flowers
nor even a diamond ring;
it's not a "warm fuzzy" feeling
nor a trinket to which one clings.
It isn't sweet words of endearment
nor whispers in one's ear:
it isn't selfish nor boastful
nor built upon doubt and fear.
But love is compassion in work clothes
and going the extra mile;
it's sacrifice made without fanfare
and bearing pain with a smile.
Love's speaking when words will encourage
but silence when words would be rude;
it's getting involved when it's helpful —
not acting when works would intrude.
In summary, love's not self-centered —
it's giving at any cost;
it is Jesus our Lord leaving Heaven
to die upon Calvary's cross!

I Can Count on You

Sometimes life brings fierce trials and pain
and no relief's in view —
but in those times of deep distress
I've learned to call on You.

Sometimes You take the pain away —
sometimes You bring me through;
sometimes You say, "Child, don't despair —
I've not forgotten you."

At times I wonder if You hear —
at times I ask You, "Why?"...
and Lord, You know that there are times
when all I do is cry.

But Lord, no matter what may come
one thing's forever true;
when all seems lost and life o'erwhelms
I can still count on You.

A Puzzle

My heavy heart cries out, "Lord, why?"
and I find it hard to pray;
when friends ask how I'm doing
I don't know what to say.

For my life seems but a puzzle
that makes no sense to me
and when I look it over
one piece is all I see.

But God holds all the pieces
secure within His hand;
He's placing each and every one —
tho' I don't understand.

He's caref'lly planned my picture
in its entirety,
so I will trust His love to choose
what He'll make of me.

At His Best

When I think of what God's done
I surely am impressed;
He made the stars, the moon, the Earth —
man, and all the rest.
He set up bounds the seas can't pass
upon their sandy breasts
and when He painted skies of blue
God was at His best.
The shepherds' song, the wise men's star,
the tree on Calv'ry's crest —
each of these and more God made
when He was at His best.
But greater far was what God did
when I was at my worst:
He called my name and offered me —
full pardon from sin's curse.
I claimed the blood He shed for me
repented of my sins...
surrendered worry, fear, and strife
to gain His peace within.
Now He guides me with His Word
through all life's trials and tests
and tho' I fail, God's ever true:
He's always at His best!

The Seductress

It seems she's won.
Alcohol has staked her claim on your heart and soul
and convinced you that you can't live without her.
She tantalizes you with promises of escape from the pain of life
and yet it is she that holds you captive.
You don't see her for who she is
because
she deceives and manipulates.
She stalks you by day
and her pleas for attention wake you in the night.
She steals your ability to reason
and to trust.
She vows she'll make you happy
but plagues you with an ever-growing emptiness
that you try in vain to fill.
You believe her enticing words
and exchange your dignity
for moments of fleeting pleasure.
Although she assaults you with regret and dashed hopes...
you continue to be faithful to her.
It seems she's won.
You would do anything for her.
You've walked away from those who loved you
and you continue to believe her when she tells you
that no one and nothing
can meet your needs like she can.
You can't see that her aim is to wreck your life.
It really does seem she's won.
But she doesn't know that there's Someone
Who truly loves you...
Someone Who is willing and able to break
the chains that so fiercely bind you

and Who longs to set you free
to become all you can be.
That Someone is He to Whom nothing is impossible.
I pray that your eyes will be opened to the reality of His love
and that you'll see your captor for who she is —
a seductress set on your destruction.
I believe that someday my prayers will be answered.
And Dear One, be assured,
although this seductress may now appear to be the victor —
deep in my heart I know
that
it only seems she has won.

Heaven's Rocking Chair

If I could bring back yesterday
I'd spend it all with you —
and I wouldn't take for granted
anything we'd say or do.
For Little One, my world collapsed
when I found that you were gone;
I kept hoping this an awful dream
and I'd wake to find you home.
But it's not a dream, it's much too real —
grief's pain won't go away...
and I wish that we could share again
some carefree happy days.
Then we'd take a walk, and laugh and talk —
and I'd hold you close to me...
I'd cherish every smile you'd smile
and be thankful as could be.
But wishing doesn't make it so —
tho' wishes I don't lack —
so I'll have to live with memories
for I cannot bring you back.
Yet it seems I hear the angels sing
that you're where you're meant to be —
and I can hardly wait, 'til in God's time,
in Heav'n you'll welcome me.
'Til then from grief I'll seek relief
as I kneel in fervent prayer —
and picture Jesus rocking you
in Heaven's rocking chair.

To My Son

Safely stored in the depths of my heart
are treasures money can't buy —
both mem'ries still in the making
and cherished ones gone by...
of a wobbly boy who took your first steps
as you held to your mommy's hand
and wore on your face a sunshine smile
as you played in the surf and the sand.
I blinked and you were a tow-headed lad
playing ball of all kinds with your team...
a sweet-natured guy that everyone loved
setting goals and claiming your dreams.
Time raced on by as I questioned just where
too quickly my young boy had gone;
in his place stood a man, a husband and dad
confident, handsome and strong...
Compassionate, generous, dependable, too,
hard-working, funny, and smart;
wherever life takes you, wherever God leads
I'll hold you close in my heart.
I pray that you know how thankful I am
that God made me the one
to love, teach, and raise you, and don't ever doubt
I'm proud of my wonderful son!

My Friend

True friendship is a priceless gift
that weaves two lives together
making each stronger and richer
than either could be alone.
It is the sharing of everyday happenings
and of incredible moments
that take one's breath away.
It is acceptance of another
and being oneself with no pretense
and no strings attached.
Few ever know it
but
because of you
I do.
You have been there for me —
cheering me on when I've struggled...
lifting me up when life has beaten me down...
and calming me when I've felt overwhelmed by circumstances.
You've rejoiced with me
laughed with me
wept with me
and endured with me.
You've held my hand (and my heart)
during some of the blackest days of my life
and
have often reminded me that there's never a time when God isn't God;
He makes no mistakes
He's in control
He has a plan.
You've given me courage to face whatever waits ahead.
You are — and will always be —
a big part of who I am.

Thank you for your prayers
your loyalty
and
your love.
I will be forever grateful that God placed you in my life
and made you
(for now and all eternity)
my friend.

Index

About the Author

Joyce Royals came to know the Lord at an early age and has been actively involved in church all of her life. Changing careers with family needs, she has been a nurse, a schoolteacher, and has worked in the business world.

She has a passion for writing, teaching adult Sunday School, and spending time with family and friends. A retired pastor's wife, she enjoys being actively involved in and supportive of the ministry of her husband, Andrew (Andy).

They are both natives of NC and currently reside in High Point, NC. They have two grown children (Tina and Steve), six grandchildren, and a grand-dog.

Contact Joyce:
jbrmomaw@gmail.com